The Road to Triumph

A Businessman's Journey

Sanchith G

Table of Contents

Part 1: The Dream

Chapter 1: Beginnings

Chapter 2: The First Steps

Chapter 3: The Mentor

Part 2: The Struggles

Chapter 4: The First Failure

Chapter 5: Rethinking the Business Model

Chapter 6: The Setback

Part 3: The Turning Point

Chapter 7: The Breakthrough Idea

Chapter 8: Building a Strong Team

Chapter 9: Scaling Up

Part 4: The Impact

Chapter 10: The Ethical Dilemma

Chapter 11: The Crisis

Chapter 12: The Expansion

Part 5: Legacy

Chapter 13: Giving Back

Chapter 14: The Full Circle

Chapter 15: The Legacy Continues

Part 1: The Dream

Chapter 1: Beginnings

Alex Hartley had always been the kind of person who saw the world not as it was, but as it could be. He could picture a future where technology and human ingenuity came together to solve the biggest challenges facing society. But his path toward that future had yet to take shape. At twenty-five, fresh out of college with a degree in engineering, Alex was full of ideas, dreams, and ambition—but he didn't have the slightest clue where to start.

He stood on the balcony of his small apartment in downtown Philadelphia, staring out at the skyline. The city was alive, pulsating with energy, but in the midst of it, Alex felt like an invisible speck in a world full of giants. His friends had landed jobs at established tech firms, secure in their paths toward comfortable careers. But Alex had always been different. He had an unshakable belief that he could create something of his own—something that could change the world.

It had started as a simple idea during his final year of college. The idea came to him in one of those half-asleep moments in the middle of the night, when your mind races and your body refuses to rest. He had been tinkering with a project, trying to design a more intuitive form of wearable technology. Something that wasn't just functional but had the power to change the way people lived—make them more connected, more mindful, and more efficient.

What if technology could truly enhance the way we experience the world? he thought, scribbling down notes in the dark.

The initial concept was crude, just a few scribbles on a napkin. But it burned inside him like an ember that wouldn't go out. As the days passed, the idea began to take shape in his mind. Wearable devices that didn't just monitor health but adapted to your lifestyle, offering real-time suggestions for improvement. A product that merged technology and personal well-being in a way that no one had done before.

It sounded ambitious. Maybe even crazy. But Alex wasn't deterred. He knew that big ideas were often the most challenging ones. And if he could make it work—if he could bring that idea to life—he would be one step closer to proving that the world was ready for change.

The first step was finding a way to fund his dream. He had a few thousand dollars saved up from a summer internship, but that wouldn't get him very far. He knew he would need investors, backing, and a team. But how could someone like him—someone with no business experience and no track record—convince anyone to believe in him?

As the weeks passed, Alex buried himself in research. He spent countless nights at his desk, scanning through articles, watching YouTube videos, and reading books about how to start a business. The process was both exhilarating and daunting. He began to understand the language of business: market analysis, customer demographics, and value propositions. It was a whole new world, one that seemed foreign compared to the comfortable, theoretical world of engineering he had left behind.

But the more Alex learned, the more convinced he became that his idea could work. He crafted a business plan, focusing on his product's uniqueness: wearable technology that not only tracked fitness and health metrics but helped users improve their lives by providing real-time, personalized insights. A device that was more than a gadget—it was a companion.

The problem was, Alex didn't know the first thing about pitching a business plan. He had no experience raising funds, no connections to investors, and no industry credentials to back up his idea. But he wasn't going to let that stop him.

The Pitch

On a crisp, cool morning in October, Alex found himself in a coffee shop on the outskirts of the city, his hands clammy as he waited for the first of several meetings he had scheduled with potential investors. The room was filled with the clatter of laptops and the hum of conversation, but Alex's focus was narrow. He had his business plan in hand, his pitch rehearsed, and his heart racing in his chest.

This is it, he thought. *This is where it all starts.*

He checked the time—ten minutes until the meeting. Alex took a deep breath, his mind reviewing the key points: product uniqueness, market demand, scalability, and the financial projections. He had spent weeks perfecting his pitch, practicing in front of mirrors, friends, and anyone who would listen. Now, all he needed was one break, one chance to prove he wasn't just another dreamer.

The door opened with a soft chime, and a man in his mid-forties walked in, his sharp suit cutting through the sea of casual attire like a knife. His name was Vincent Lang, a well-known investor in the tech space, and Alex had done everything he could to secure this meeting.

Lang's piercing gaze met Alex's as he took a seat across from him. The investor didn't waste time on pleasantries. He placed a briefcase on the table, opened it, and took out a laptop.

"So, you have five minutes. Tell me why I should care about your idea," Lang said, his voice deep and direct.

Alex's stomach flipped. Five minutes? Was that all? He had spent weeks preparing for this moment, but now that it was here, the pressure felt almost suffocating.

He cleared his throat and began. "I believe that wearable technology can go beyond fitness tracking. It can be a tool for improving overall well-being, not just tracking metrics but actually helping people optimize their daily lives."

Lang raised an eyebrow, clearly intrigued. Alex continued, outlining the idea, the market, and the potential for growth. As he spoke, the words flowed more easily. He felt the connection between himself and the idea he was presenting. This wasn't just a business—this was his passion. He had poured his soul into every detail.

When Alex finished, there was a brief silence. Lang sat back in his chair, tapping his fingers on the table.

"I like the idea," Lang said, his voice thoughtful. "But you're young. You have no experience running a business. What makes you think you can pull this off?"

Alex's heart sank. He had been waiting for this moment of doubt, but hearing it out loud made it feel even more real. "I may not have experience, but I have something more important: determination and the willingness to learn," Alex replied, his voice steady. "I'm not just asking for money. I'm asking for a partnership. I want to build something together, to change the way people think about technology and well-being."

Lang's expression softened slightly. "I'll tell you what, kid. I'll take a closer look at your plan. You've got guts. I'll give you that. But don't expect anything until I see results. In the world of business, results are the only thing that matter."

The meeting ended with a handshake, and Alex left the coffee shop feeling a strange mix of hope and uncertainty. He knew this was just the beginning, and the road ahead would be filled with more rejections, more uncertainty. But for the first time, Alex felt like his dream could become a reality.

Back to the Drawing Board

Despite the cautious optimism from the meeting, Alex knew he wasn't out of the woods. He had to prove his concept, refine his product, and build a team that could bring the vision to life. The next few weeks were a blur of coding, prototyping, and learning the ins and outs of running a business. Every night, he stayed up late, reading, coding, and tinkering.

But as the days passed, Alex realized that creating a business wasn't just about having a great idea. It was about managing expectations—his own and others'. The investors wanted to see a finished product, not just promises. They wanted data, not dreams.

And that's when it hit him: he wasn't just building a product. He was building a brand, a reputation, and a business from the ground up. The road ahead would be long, but with determination and a willingness to learn, he would take each step with purpose.

As he sat at his desk one evening, Alex opened his laptop and looked at the business plan once more. The numbers, the projections, the challenges—they all seemed so daunting. But in the center of the plan, one line stood out: *Innovation is born from persistence, not perfection.*

With a renewed sense of purpose, Alex got to work.

Chapter 2: The First Steps

The days after Alex's meeting with Vincent Lang felt like a blur. His mind raced with possibilities, and his heart burned with the same intensity that had first sparked the idea for his business. But the reality of turning a dream into a viable company was beginning to settle in. He had a solid concept, a few investors showing interest, and an ever-growing list of things to do.

One thing became immediately clear: he needed a team.

Alex wasn't naïve enough to think he could do it all alone. He had technical expertise, sure, but he was learning quickly that running a business was about much more than just creating a product. Marketing, finance, legalities, and partnerships were areas where he had little to no experience. He needed people who knew how to navigate these complex waters, people who shared his vision and were willing to take the same risks.

The first person he turned to was Emily Sanders, a classmate from college who had graduated with a degree in business administration. Emily had always been a practical thinker, grounded in reality, and that was exactly what Alex needed. She was a natural organizer and had a knack for breaking down complex problems into manageable steps.

Over coffee one morning, Alex laid out his vision for the business. He spoke about the potential of wearable technology, how it could be more than just a fitness tracker, and how his product could change people's lives. Emily listened intently, nodding as she absorbed every detail.

"I like it, Alex. I really do," she said thoughtfully. "But I'm going to be honest with you. It's a big undertaking. You're going to need a lot more than just a good product. You'll need a business model that works, a plan for scaling, and—most importantly—a market. Who are you selling to?"

Alex had anticipated these questions. "The target market is anyone who values health and productivity—busy professionals, fitness enthusiasts, and even people looking for self-improvement. But it's more than that. This is a lifestyle product. It's about building a relationship between the user and their device. Think of it like a personal assistant, but for your health and well-being."

Emily's eyes sparkled with interest. "You're going to need a strong brand identity, then. Something that sets you apart in a crowded market. How do you plan to create that?"

Alex paused. That was the question he had been grappling with. He hadn't yet figured out how to position his product in a way that made it stand out from the sea of fitness trackers already on the market.

"I'm not sure yet," Alex admitted, "but I'm willing to figure it out. That's why I need you, Emily. I need someone who can help me make sense of all this business jargon and turn it into a plan we can execute."

Emily smiled. "Well, I can't promise miracles, but I'll help you get started. I'll put together a market research plan, figure out what our competitors are doing, and see if we can identify any gaps in the market. You'll need to create a prototype, right?"

Alex nodded. "That's the next step. I have the basic concept, but I need to build the first working version. I have a few ideas, but I need the right equipment and materials. I also need to make sure it's functional—this can't just be a gimmick."

Emily tapped her fingers on her coffee cup thoughtfully. "Okay. Let's get to work."

Building the Prototype

With Emily on board, Alex turned his attention to the technical side of things. He spent long hours in his small apartment, poring over design documents, studying circuit boards, and soldering components together. It was the work he was most familiar with—the work that had always brought him a sense of peace. But now, as he labored over the prototype, he knew that this was just the beginning. He wasn't just building a piece of technology; he was building the future of his company.

Days turned into weeks. There were setbacks—wires that didn't connect properly, software that crashed, and ideas that didn't quite work the way he imagined. But Alex had come to realize that setbacks were part of the process. The road to success was never a straight line.

As the weeks passed, Emily began to compile her market research. She identified several key competitors in the wearable tech space, including established companies like Fitbit and Apple. But she also identified gaps in the market. While many fitness trackers focused on health metrics, none of them offered a truly personalized experience. None of them adapted to the user's lifestyle in the way Alex envisioned.

The more they dug into the market, the more Emily's confidence grew. "You're onto something here," she said one evening after reviewing the data. "There's definitely a niche for a product like this. But we need a killer feature—something that really sets you apart."

Alex thought for a moment. He had always believed in the idea of personalized wellness, but there was a key piece missing. "What if we make it about more than just health? What if we add a social element—something that connects users with others who are on the same journey of self-improvement? People want to feel like they're part of something bigger. Maybe we could build a community around the product."

Emily nodded. "I like it. A product that's not just functional, but also part of a lifestyle. A product that makes people feel connected to a community of like-minded individuals. That's the kind of branding we need."

The Pitch to Investors

With the prototype nearing completion and Emily's research providing the foundation for a solid business model, Alex felt ready to take the next step: approaching investors again.

This time, he wasn't walking into the room with just a dream. He had a plan. He had a prototype. And most importantly, he had a clear vision of where the business could go.

The second meeting with Vincent Lang was scheduled for a Wednesday morning. Alex arrived early, pacing outside the office building, reviewing his pitch. He was no longer the unsure, naïve entrepreneur who had walked into the coffee shop weeks ago. Now, he was armed with knowledge, a product, and a solid plan for growth.

When Lang arrived, Alex wasted no time in presenting his ideas. He outlined the market research, the prototype, and the key differentiators of his product. He spoke about the potential for growth, the ways in which the product could scale, and how he planned to build a loyal customer base.

Lang listened intently, occasionally asking questions, but Alex could tell he was intrigued. When Alex finished his pitch, there was a long pause. Lang leaned back in his chair, tapping his fingers thoughtfully on the desk.

"I've seen a lot of pitches, Alex. But I have to admit, this is different," Lang said. "You've put in the work. You have a plan. And you're offering something more than just a product—you're offering a vision. I'm interested. But I need to see how this plays out in the real world. How quickly can you get this to market?"

Alex's heart skipped a beat. This was it. The moment he had been working toward. "We're almost there," Alex said, his voice steady. "We've got the prototype. We're finalizing the software. With your backing, we can take this to the next level. We'll launch a crowdfunding campaign to build buzz, and then we'll hit the market hard with a targeted ad campaign."

Lang nodded, his expression serious. "Alright, Alex. I'm in. Let's see what you can do."

Alex couldn't help but smile. It was a small victory, but it was a victory nonetheless. With Lang's backing, he now had the resources to push forward—no more doubts, no more uncertainty.

The real work was just beginning.

Chapter 3: The Mentor

The road ahead for Alex seemed to stretch endlessly, a mixture of exhilarating highs and frustrating lows. The early days of starting his business were both thrilling and exhausting. He found himself juggling a thousand tasks at once—finalizing the product design, researching marketing strategies, and navigating the complex landscape of investors, legal paperwork, and supply chains. There were days when it felt like the weight of the world was on his shoulders, and the constant pressure to succeed started to take a toll on him.

One afternoon, as he sat in his cramped office staring at his computer screen, his phone buzzed with a text from Emily. *"I've set up a meeting with someone who can help you. Trust me, you need this."*

Alex frowned, momentarily unsure what Emily meant. He wasn't sure he could take on any more commitments, but then again, he couldn't afford to turn away opportunities either. He responded with a simple, *"Who?"*

Her reply came almost instantly: *"A mentor. Someone who has been through the grind and knows the ropes. I really think you'll learn a lot from him."*

The word *mentor* felt like a foreign concept to Alex. He had always believed that success came from self-reliance and hard work, not leaning on others for guidance. But deep down, he knew he could use some wisdom, especially when it came to the intricacies of scaling his business. The idea of someone guiding him through the complexities of entrepreneurship seemed appealing, but he still wasn't sure what to expect.

"Alright, set it up," Alex texted back.

Meeting The Mentor

The following Thursday, Alex found himself walking through the doors of a sleek downtown office building. It was the kind of place that reeked of success—modern design, polished floors, and a view of the city skyline that screamed wealth and ambition. Alex felt a pang of self-doubt, unsure whether he belonged in this world of polished suits and corporate meetings.

He was greeted by a secretary and ushered into a conference room where an older man was already seated. The man looked to be in his late fifties, dressed casually yet with an air of authority that seemed to command respect. His salt-and-pepper hair was neatly combed, and his face, though lined with age, radiated wisdom.

"Alex," the man said with a warm smile as he stood to shake his hand. "It's good to finally meet you."

"Thank you for taking the time to meet with me," Alex replied, taking a seat across from him.

"Of course," the man said, sitting back down and folding his hands. "I hear you're starting something exciting. Tell me about it."

Alex launched into the story of his wearable technology business, his vision, the challenges he'd faced, and the progress he'd made. As he spoke, he felt a bit of nervous energy but also a growing sense of purpose. This wasn't just some casual conversation—it was a chance to connect with someone who had walked the path before him.

The older man listened intently, nodding along, but his expression remained neutral, as though assessing every word. When Alex finished, there was a brief silence. The man leaned forward, his eyes sharp.

"Your idea is good, Alex," he said, his tone measured. "But you're not just building a product—you're building a business. And that's where most entrepreneurs go wrong. They think that if they have a great idea, everything else will fall into place. But the reality is, running a business requires a different set of skills."

Alex nodded, trying to keep his emotions in check. "I know. That's why I'm here."

The man smiled again, this time with a hint of approval. "Good. My name's Thomas Blackwood. I've been in the business world for over thirty years. I've made my share of mistakes, learned from them, and built multiple companies from the ground up. Now, I spend most of my time mentoring entrepreneurs like you. You see, it's not enough to have passion. You need to learn how to harness it. The right strategy, the right decisions—they come from knowledge and experience. I'm here to help you with that."

Alex was intrigued. "So, what do you suggest I do first?"

Thomas paused, his gaze intense. "Let's start by talking about your business model."

The Business Model

As the meeting progressed, Alex quickly realized how much he had yet to learn. Thomas dissected his business model with a critical eye, pointing out areas where Alex had overlooked key details and others where he had made assumptions that weren't grounded in reality.

"You've got a good product, but your market strategy needs more work," Thomas explained. "You're focusing too much on features and not enough on how those features translate to benefits for your customers. A good product speaks for itself, but a great business knows how to communicate that value. You need to define your customer segment clearly. Who are they? What do they need? What problems are you solving for them?"

Alex felt his mind whirring as Thomas's words sank in. It was all starting to make sense. He'd been so focused on building the product that he hadn't fully considered the bigger picture—the marketing, the customer, the long-term vision of his company.

"We're aiming for professionals and fitness enthusiasts," Alex explained. "People who want to be more productive and live healthier lifestyles."

Thomas leaned back in his chair, tapping his fingers on the table. "That's a broad group. You need to niche down. Find a specific pain point that no one else is addressing. If you try to appeal to everyone, you'll end up appealing to no one."

It was a harsh reality check, but Alex could see the wisdom in Thomas's advice. Every successful business, he realized, had a niche—something that set it apart from the competition.

The Tough Love

The next few meetings with Thomas were a whirlwind of advice, critique, and tough love. Thomas didn't sugarcoat anything. He pushed Alex to confront his weaknesses, especially when it came to his understanding of finances, operations, and scaling a business.

"You're burning through your funds too quickly," Thomas pointed out one day, after reviewing Alex's financial projections. "And you're relying too heavily on investors to fund your growth. That's not a sustainable model. You need to figure out how to generate revenue early, even if it's just small amounts at first. Bootstrap your way to success, then use that momentum to attract more investors."

Alex felt overwhelmed, but he appreciated Thomas's blunt approach. It forced him to think critically about his choices. Thomas didn't just tell him what to do—he made him think for himself, teaching him to see the pitfalls before they became disasters.

"Don't be afraid to fail," Thomas told him during one particularly tough meeting. "You're going to make mistakes, but that's how you learn. The real failure is giving up because it gets hard. You need to be in this for the long haul."

The Turning Point

Months passed, and Alex slowly began to apply the lessons he was learning from Thomas. He refined his business model, adjusted his marketing approach, and, most importantly, started thinking like an entrepreneur. He learned to make decisions based on data, not just gut feelings, and he understood the importance of every dollar spent in his business. He began to see his vision more clearly—not as a lofty dream, but as a series of actionable steps that could lead him to success.

One day, after months of work, Alex sat across from Thomas in a small café, feeling the weight of the journey behind him. He had made mistakes, corrected them, and learned more than he ever thought possible.

"I think we're ready," Alex said, his voice steady. "I think we have everything in place to launch."

Thomas smiled, a knowing look in his eyes. "You've come a long way, Alex. But remember, the real work starts now. Keep learning. Keep growing. And never forget—success isn't about avoiding mistakes. It's about learning from them and never giving up."

With those words, Alex understood. The mentor wasn't just giving him answers—he was teaching him how to find them himself. He was showing Alex that the true path to success was a journey, not a destination.

Part 2: The Struggles

Chapter 4: The First Failure

After months of intense preparation, strategizing, and countless hours of hard work, Alex felt as though he was finally on the verge of achieving something monumental. His product was ready, his business model had been refined, and the marketing plan was set in motion. The future seemed bright, and for the first time in a long while, Alex allowed himself to feel the warmth of hope.

The day he launched his wearable tech product was the culmination of every sleepless night, every strategic meeting, every conversation with his mentor, Thomas. He'd put everything on the line—the savings, the borrowed money, the hours spent perfecting the device. The website went live, the social media posts were shared, and the emails went out. The response, or so Alex thought, would be swift and overwhelming. His inbox was ready to fill with inquiries, sales orders, and positive feedback.

But the next morning, Alex opened his email with anticipation—only to find nothing.

No orders.

No inquiries.

Not even a single comment.

Alex sat at his desk, staring blankly at the screen. His mind raced through every possibility. Did he miss something? Was the product not good enough? Had the marketing not worked? Surely, he thought, something would happen. But the day dragged on, and the silence continued to haunt him.

By the end of the week, there was still no response. No orders had come in, and the social media engagement was lackluster at best. The few people who did interact with his posts seemed disinterested, leaving vague comments and forgetting the product existed altogether.

The Weight of Disappointment

It was on that fourth day, sitting at his desk and staring at his barren sales dashboard, that Alex felt the crushing weight of failure for the first time. His optimism had been shattered. His vision had been so clear, but now, it seemed like the universe was mocking him.

The self-doubt crept in slowly at first—quiet whispers in the back of his mind. *Maybe this was all a mistake. Maybe I'm not cut out for this after all.*

He tried to distract himself with other tasks, but nothing could shake the gnawing feeling of failure. He had worked so hard, had put everything on the line, and now, it felt like the dream was slipping through his fingers. It wasn't just about the product. It was about his identity as an entrepreneur, his belief in his vision, and the trust he had put in others.

Alex felt alone, like he had ventured into unknown territory and had no way of finding his way back. The calls with Thomas had become less frequent. He didn't want to admit to his mentor that things weren't going as planned, so he kept quiet, hoping the problem would resolve itself. But the silence from customers only grew louder.

One evening, Alex sat on the couch in his small apartment, his laptop closed and the lights dimmed. He replayed every decision, every step, every strategy he had executed. Had he made a mistake somewhere? Was there a flaw in his business model? Should he have chosen a different market or approach?

His phone buzzed, pulling him from his spiral. It was Emily, his long-time friend and one of his earliest supporters.

"Hey, how's everything going? I've been following the launch, and I know you've been working so hard on this. You're doing great!"

For a moment, Alex sat there staring at the text, unsure how to respond. He didn't feel great. He didn't feel like anything was going well. But he had learned to be diplomatic in these situations, to wear a mask and tell people what they wanted to hear.

"Thanks, Emily. Things are… moving along. I'll keep you posted."

That was all he could muster. He couldn't bring himself to be vulnerable, not when he felt like he had already failed.

Facing the Music

The following week, Alex met with Thomas again, his mentor sensing that something wasn't quite right. He invited Alex to his office, and the moment they sat down, Alex couldn't hold it in any longer.

"I'm failing," Alex admitted, his voice tight with frustration. "I thought everything was ready, but no one is buying the product. It's not getting any traction. I don't know what I missed."

Thomas leaned back in his chair, his hands folded in front of him. "Failure is part of the process, Alex. It's not the end of your journey, it's just a part of it. You've got to reframe this. You're not failing, you're learning."

Alex let out a bitter laugh. "Learning what? That I'm in over my head? That I should've stayed in my safe job?"

Thomas looked at him with a mixture of empathy and firmness. "No. You're learning how to overcome setbacks. Every entrepreneur has faced this moment, every single one. What separates the successful ones from the others is how they respond when things don't go as planned."

Alex rubbed his temples, the weight of his frustration making it hard to focus. "But how do I respond? I've put everything into this. How do I turn it around when it feels like no one cares?"

"Let's talk about your strategy," Thomas said calmly. "I'm going to give you some tough love here, Alex. Your marketing was all wrong. You went too broad, too fast. Your message didn't connect with your audience the way it should have."

Alex was quiet for a moment, taking in the criticism. "So, what do I do now?"

Thomas smiled slightly, as if this was a turning point he had been waiting for. "Now, you go back to basics. You identify your target market and focus on creating a message that speaks directly to their needs. You've got a great product, but you need to communicate that in a way that resonates with the right people. You need to create an emotional connection, not just a transaction."

Rebuilding and Pivoting

Alex took Thomas's advice to heart. Over the next few weeks, he shifted his focus. He identified a smaller, more specific audience—fitness enthusiasts who were looking for cutting-edge ways to track their progress. Rather than just selling the product's features, he reworked his messaging to focus on how the product could help them achieve their fitness goals more effectively and efficiently.

He also sought out customer feedback. He reached out to those who had shown interest during the initial launch but had not yet made a purchase. Through candid conversations, Alex began to realize that people were excited about the idea, but they didn't understand why it was different from other products already on the market.

With this newfound insight, Alex revamped his marketing materials, reworked his social media campaigns, and even reached out to a few influencers in the fitness space for partnerships. Slowly, he started to see results. The first few sales trickled in, then picked up pace, and for the first time, he felt a glimmer of hope again.

A Lesson in Resilience

The experience of failure had been painful, but it was also transformative. Alex learned that failure wasn't something to fear—it was a necessary part of growth. He learned to adapt, to pivot, and to refine his strategies based on real-world feedback. Most importantly, he learned that setbacks didn't define him. His response to them did.

As Alex sat in his office weeks later, watching his product gain more traction and seeing customers' positive feedback, he knew one thing for sure: he was no longer afraid to fail. In fact, he welcomed it as a teacher.

Chapter 5: Rethinking the Business Model

The weeks following Alex's disappointing product launch were a whirlwind of self-reflection, reevaluation, and hard lessons. While his initial failure stung, it also provided him with a valuable opportunity to pause and reflect on his approach. He had always believed that success was the outcome of hard work and perseverance, but now he realized that it wasn't just about putting in the hours—it was about working smarter and being willing to adapt when things weren't going as planned.

Alex sat at his desk one morning, staring at his computer screen. The numbers on his sales dashboard were better, but still nowhere near where he had hoped they would be. The product was getting some traction, but not enough to sustain the growth he had envisioned. He had been so focused on launching the product and getting it out there that he hadn't paid enough attention to the finer details. The feedback he had gathered from customers was helpful, but there was still a nagging feeling that something fundamental was missing.

His phone buzzed, pulling him out of his thoughts. It was a text from Thomas.

"Let's meet up. I think it's time we take a deep dive into your business model."

Alex had learned to trust Thomas's instincts. He set aside the feelings of doubt that still lingered from the launch and agreed to meet at his mentor's office.

The Meeting

When Alex walked into Thomas's office, he immediately sensed a shift. This wasn't going to be a casual check-in—it was time for a serious conversation.

"Alex," Thomas began, his tone both stern and supportive, "you've got a great product, but it's clear that your current business model isn't working as well as it should. You've been focusing a lot on product development and marketing, but you've neglected one crucial thing: your value proposition."

Alex frowned. "What do you mean?"

"Think about it," Thomas continued. "You've been targeting a broad audience, trying to appeal to everyone. But you're not just selling a product; you're selling a solution. The question is, who has the problem that your product solves?"

Alex sat back in his chair, thinking carefully. "Fitness enthusiasts. They need better ways to track their progress. That's who I'm targeting."

Thomas nodded but pressed on. "That's a start, but you need to dig deeper. What are the specific needs of those fitness enthusiasts? Are they professionals or beginners? What pain points are they experiencing that your product can fix? Your value proposition isn't just about the product—it's about the transformation you offer."

Alex had heard the term "value proposition" before, but now it clicked in a way it hadn't before. The product itself was great, but what was missing was the narrative around it—the story of how it could change lives.

"I get it," Alex said, starting to see the bigger picture. "It's not enough to just sell a product. I need to show how it's going to make a difference for my customers."

Thomas smiled. "Exactly. But it's more than just finding your target audience. You also need to rethink your pricing strategy, your distribution channels, and how you're positioning the product in the market."

Reevaluating the Approach

Over the next few days, Alex took a hard look at his business model from top to bottom. He began by revisiting his target market, trying to refine it further. He realized that, while fitness enthusiasts were a large group, there were segments within that group he had overlooked—beginners who were just getting into fitness, for instance, and busy professionals who struggled to maintain consistency in their workouts.

Alex decided to narrow his focus even further, deciding to target people who had a strong desire to improve their health but didn't have the time or experience to track their progress effectively. They were overwhelmed by the sheer volume of information out there and needed a simple, easy-to-use solution.

His next step was to revisit his pricing strategy. The initial launch had offered his product at a premium price, positioning it as a high-end gadget for serious fitness enthusiasts. But the feedback from customers suggested that many potential buyers felt it was too expensive for what they perceived to be a novelty item.

Alex's thoughts turned to how he could make the product more accessible. He didn't want to compromise on quality, but perhaps offering a tiered pricing model could help. He considered a basic version of the product with fewer features and a lower price point, which would appeal to those who were just starting their fitness journeys. Then, he could offer premium features as part of an upsell to more serious users later on. This would allow him to capture a broader range of customers without alienating any group.

Next, he thought about distribution. Initially, he had relied heavily on his online store, hoping that a direct-to-consumer model would be enough to generate sales. But he realized that he hadn't explored all possible sales channels. What if he could partner with fitness clubs, gyms, or personal trainers who could recommend the product to their clients? What if he could get the product into retail stores, where customers could see and touch it before making a purchase?

Finally, Alex revisited his marketing approach. His initial campaigns had been too focused on features and specifications. While these elements were important, they didn't speak to the emotional side of the customer's journey. He needed to focus on the transformation his product could provide—helping people reach their fitness goals more easily, stay motivated, and feel more in control of their health.

Testing the New Model

Armed with these new insights, Alex made changes to his business model and prepared to test them on a small scale. He revamped his website with a clearer value proposition that spoke directly to the pain points of his target audience. He updated his product offerings, introducing the tiered pricing structure, and he started reaching out to local gyms and fitness influencers to explore distribution and marketing partnerships.

The early results were promising. Alex saw a slight uptick in website traffic, and more importantly, his conversions started to improve. The feedback from customers was more positive, with many praising the simpler pricing options and the product's ability to help them track their progress more effectively. It wasn't an overnight success, but it was a step in the right direction.

He continued to test and refine the model, learning from his customers' feedback and adjusting his approach as needed. The process wasn't easy, but Alex was beginning to see that true success wasn't about sticking rigidly to a plan—it was about being adaptable, listening to your customers, and constantly evolving.

The Power of Pivoting

As the weeks went by, Alex began to understand the true power of pivoting. His willingness to rethink his business model and make the necessary adjustments had set him on the path to growth. But more importantly, he had learned to embrace the fluid nature of entrepreneurship. It wasn't about finding a single formula for success—it was about continually adapting, learning from mistakes, and improving over time.

Thomas had been right: the journey to success was rarely a straight line. It was filled with bumps, turns, and detours. But with each challenge, Alex was becoming stronger, more resilient, and more prepared for whatever came next.

As Alex looked at his growing customer base, he realized that he wasn't just building a business—he was building something that could make a real difference in people's lives. And that, he knew, was the key to long-term success.

Chapter 6: The Setback

Just when things were beginning to look up for Alex, fate seemed to throw another obstacle in his path. The new business model he had spent weeks refining was gaining traction, and the sales were steadily rising. But in the midst of his momentum, he faced an unexpected setback—a competitor had entered the market, and they were coming in hard and fast.

It all started with a phone call early one Monday morning. Alex was sitting in his office, sipping coffee and reviewing the latest sales figures when his phone buzzed. It was Sarah, his marketing director.

"Alex, I need you to check this out. It's urgent," she said, her tone urgent yet calm.

Alex immediately opened his email, and there, at the top of his inbox, was a link to a press release. His heart skipped a beat as he read the headline:

New Competitor in the Fitness Tech Space: Introducing a Game-Changing Tracker at an Unbeatable Price.

His eyes scanned the article. The company had just launched a similar product to Alex's, one that had all the features he had painstakingly developed, and—this was the kicker—at a significantly lower price point. They also had a slick marketing campaign that seemed to be everywhere—social media, influencers, and even in fitness magazines. The new competitor had already begun to steal attention from Alex's target market, and the buzz around their product was undeniable.

Alex sat back in his chair, feeling the weight of the situation pressing down on him. It was as if everything he had worked for had been upended in a matter of hours. The competitor's product had all the bells and whistles his had—only at a fraction of the price. They had a bigger marketing budget, a more extensive distribution network, and, most importantly, a faster time to market.

It wasn't long before the sales numbers for Alex's product started to dip. He knew it was a direct result of the competitor's launch. His phone rang again. It was Thomas.

"How are things going, Alex?" Thomas asked, as if sensing his unease.

"Not great," Alex admitted, staring at the screen. "We've got a competitor who's undercutting us on price and pushing hard with their marketing. I don't know how we're going to compete."

"Alright," Thomas said, his voice calm and measured. "Take a deep breath. This is the reality of business. There will always be competition, and there will always be setbacks. The question is, how are you going to respond?"

Alex thought for a moment, the frustration building within him. "I feel like everything we've worked for is slipping through our fingers. What do I do now?"

"First," Thomas replied, "you need to stop and assess the situation. The competitor's price point is a big challenge, but it's not the end of the world. There's always room for differentiation. You have to think about what makes your product unique, and how you can turn this into an advantage."

Alex took a deep breath and nodded, trying to calm his nerves. It wasn't the first time he had faced a challenge in his business journey, but this felt different. It wasn't just about adjusting his marketing or pricing strategy—it was about reevaluating everything he had built.

Reevaluating the Positioning

Alex spent the next few days in a fog of frustration and doubt. The competitor's product was slick, professional, and offered a seemingly unbeatable price. But Alex was determined not to let the setback define him. After all, he had faced failure before, and he knew that every setback was an opportunity to come out stronger.

He decided to take Thomas's advice seriously and reevaluate his product's positioning. He knew that in order to survive in the market, he had to carve out a unique space. It wasn't enough to just compete on price and features—Alex had to think beyond that. He had to remind himself why he started this business in the first place.

Late one night, after a long day of strategizing, Alex sat down to reflect on his mission. He thought about the customers he had worked with over the past few months, their success stories, and how his product had made a tangible difference in their lives. He had always wanted to help people improve their health and fitness, but he realized that his initial focus had been too narrow. It wasn't just about tracking progress—it was about empowering people to take control of their health and live fuller, more balanced lives.

The next morning, he called his team together for an emergency meeting. "We need to focus on the emotional connection we have with our customers," Alex said, his voice filled with resolve. "We're not just selling a product—we're selling a journey. We're helping people improve their lives."

Sarah, the marketing director, nodded thoughtfully. "I get it. So, we should double down on the storytelling aspect? Make it more about the experience of using the product, not just the features?"

"Exactly," Alex said. "We've been so focused on the technical side of things, but it's time to shift our narrative. We need to show our customers how we're different—not just with the product, but with the experience we offer. We're about empowerment, not just tracking."

Turning the Setback into an Advantage

As Alex and his team brainstormed ways to reposition the brand, he realized that the setback wasn't as devastating as he had originally thought. In fact, it presented an opportunity. The competitor's aggressive pricing strategy had made it clear that they were targeting the mass market, appealing to a broad audience. But Alex's product had a much more focused purpose—it wasn't just for anyone who wanted to track their fitness; it was for people who were serious about making a lasting change in their health and wellness.

The team decided to reframe their marketing message around this shift. They focused on the personal stories of their customers—how the product had helped them stay motivated, overcome setbacks, and achieve their fitness goals. They shared testimonials, not just of weight loss or muscle gain, but of people feeling empowered to live healthier, more balanced lives. They launched a campaign centered on the theme of *Transformation Through Empowerment*, emphasizing that their product was a tool to help users take control of their journey, not just track their progress.

They also refined their pricing strategy. While they couldn't compete on price alone, they knew they could offer added value in other ways. They introduced personalized coaching and customer support, creating a community around the product where users could connect with trainers, nutritionists, and other like-minded individuals. This added service became a cornerstone of their offering, setting them apart from the competitor.

Within weeks, the feedback started to shift. Customers who had been attracted to the competitor's lower price realized the true value in Alex's product—its ability to not just track progress, but to foster a deeper sense of commitment and transformation. Sales slowly but steadily began to rise again.

Lessons Learned

The setback was far from easy, but it taught Alex invaluable lessons about business and resilience. He learned that in the face of competition, it was not enough to simply copy what others were doing; he had to focus on what made his product unique and find ways to build a stronger emotional connection with his customers. It was a humbling reminder that success was never guaranteed, and that every setback carried with it the potential for growth and reinvention.

As Alex watched his business start to regain momentum, he realized that setbacks were not the end of the journey. They were merely detours—opportunities to rethink, reframe, and ultimately become stronger and more focused. He now understood that setbacks weren't failures; they were simply stepping stones to something greater.

And with that newfound perspective, Alex felt more ready than ever to face whatever challenges lay ahead.

Part 3: The Turning Point

Chapter 7: The Breakthrough Idea

After the initial shock of the competitor's launch and the subsequent efforts to reposition his brand, Alex had learned that business wasn't just about surviving the challenges—it was about thriving despite them. The new marketing campaign and the refined product offering had put him on the path to recovery, but he knew something was still missing. He had to find a way to truly distinguish his company from the competition, to offer something so unique that no one could replicate it.

It was a rainy Tuesday morning when the breakthrough idea hit him. Alex was sitting in his usual café, the one just down the street from his office. The aroma of freshly brewed coffee mingled with the chatter of other patrons. He had spent the morning going over numbers and plans, but nothing seemed to spark that spark of inspiration he so desperately needed.

Frustration began to rise as he scrolled through his phone, reading the latest headlines about his competitors' aggressive expansions. He had to do something different—something bold. That's when he heard it.

A woman at the table next to him was talking animatedly about her recent experience with a fitness app she had been using for several months. She mentioned how it had helped her stay on track with her exercise routine and how she felt more connected to her fitness goals than ever before. But then she said something that caught Alex's attention.

"I don't know," the woman said to her friend. "The tracking is great, but it's just numbers. I wish I had someone to actually talk to about it. A real person who can tell me what I'm doing right or wrong."

The woman's words resonated with Alex. He had heard this sentiment before, both from his customers and from his own experiences. While fitness tracking was valuable, many people still felt disconnected, isolated, and overwhelmed by the technical data. There was an emotional and human element missing from the experience. It wasn't enough to just offer a product that tracked progress—people wanted support, encouragement, and guidance.

That's when the idea struck him.

A Personal Touch

What if Alex's product could offer something beyond just tracking? What if it could provide personalized coaching, direct feedback, and real-time support from experts who understood the user's unique goals and struggles?

The idea was simple yet powerful: Create an integrated system where every user had access to a personal coach—someone who could help them interpret the data, make suggestions based on their individual progress, and offer real, human guidance on how to stay motivated. This coach would be available through a combination of in-app messaging, video calls, and personalized feedback loops, allowing users to feel like they weren't just another number in a sea of fitness enthusiasts.

Alex's mind raced as he began to flesh out the details of this breakthrough idea. It wasn't just about offering virtual fitness coaches—it was about creating a community. A community where users felt supported not only by the product, but by people who genuinely cared about their well-being. The more Alex thought about it, the clearer it became that this wasn't just a marketing gimmick. This was a solution to the isolation that so many people felt when it came to their fitness journeys.

He knew it would take time to build, but he was ready for the challenge. The more he imagined this new direction, the more excited he became. This was the key to setting his company apart from the competitors. It was about blending technology with a human touch—an element that no one else in the market was offering.

Implementing the Idea

The very next day, Alex called a meeting with Sarah, Thomas, and the rest of the leadership team. They gathered in the conference room, where Alex unveiled the idea that had consumed his thoughts over the past 24 hours.

"I want to introduce a new concept," Alex began, his voice full of energy. "We're going to offer every user a personalized fitness coach. Not just any coach, but one who can guide them through their journey, track their progress, and help them stay motivated. It's time to bridge the gap between data and emotional connection."

There was a moment of stunned silence in the room before Thomas spoke up. "Alex, this is huge. It's not just an app or a product—it's a service. It could change the way people view fitness apps."

Sarah nodded thoughtfully. "The idea of real, personal support could make a huge difference. But how are we going to pull this off? It's one thing to offer tracking, but how do we provide personalized coaching at scale?"

Alex smiled, feeling the excitement grow. "I've been thinking about that. We'll start by hiring certified coaches—real experts in fitness and wellness. They'll use our platform to interact with the users, give them advice, and track their progress. We'll use the app to connect them in real-time, making sure they're always available when users need them. It's the ultimate blend of technology and human expertise."

"Wow," Sarah said, looking impressed. "This could be a game-changer."

The Road to Launch

Over the next few weeks, Alex and his team worked tirelessly to bring the vision to life. They spent countless hours hiring a team of fitness coaches, nutritionists, and wellness experts. They also built out the infrastructure to support one-on-one coaching sessions, integrating video calls, chat functions, and personalized feedback systems into the app.

But as they moved forward, challenges arose. The hiring process was longer than anticipated, and the integration of the coaching features was more complicated than they had originally thought. However, with each obstacle, Alex remained resolute. He knew that this was the breakthrough he had been waiting for, and he wasn't about to let it slip away due to a few bumps in the road.

Finally, after months of hard work, the new feature was ready to launch. They rolled it out slowly, initially offering it to a select group of users in a beta test. The feedback was overwhelming. Users loved the personal connection with their coaches, and many reported feeling more motivated than ever before.

One user, a woman named Laura, shared her story in the app's feedback section. "I've tried countless fitness apps, but this one is different. The coach I've been working with has not only helped me with my workouts but has been there to support me through every obstacle. I feel like I'm not alone on this journey anymore."

The success of the beta test was just the beginning. Alex and his team quickly began ramping up their marketing efforts, promoting the personalized coaching service as the key differentiator that would set them apart from the competition.

The Impact

As the coaching service gained traction, Alex watched his company begin to thrive once more. The personalized experience resonated with users, and word quickly spread. More and more people were signing up, eager to experience the added value of having their own fitness coach. The competitor's lower-priced offering was still on the market, but it no longer seemed like the only option.

Alex had created something no one else had. And in doing so, he had transformed his business.

Lessons Learned

In the end, Alex realized that the breakthrough idea wasn't just about offering a product or service—it was about recognizing the emotional needs of his customers and meeting them with empathy and support. The success of his personalized coaching service taught him that in business, it wasn't enough to just deliver what people wanted. You had to understand what they truly needed and find innovative ways to deliver that need.

For Alex, the breakthrough idea wasn't the end—it was the beginning of a new chapter in his entrepreneurial journey. The lesson was clear: true innovation comes when you focus on solving real problems, not just capitalizing on trends.

As he sat back and reflected on the growth of his company, Alex realized that the hardest moments often lead to the most profound breakthroughs. And with that, he was ready for whatever came next.

Chapter 8: Building a Strong Team

After the breakthrough idea had successfully launched, Alex found himself riding a wave of newfound confidence. The personalized fitness coaching service had taken off, and his company was finally gaining the traction it needed. The growth was undeniable, and with it came new challenges that demanded his attention. But despite the success, Alex knew that he couldn't continue to carry the weight of the business alone.

The team he had built in the early days had been small—just a few dedicated people who had worked tirelessly alongside him through thick and thin. But as the company expanded, Alex realized that he needed to build a stronger, more capable team if they were going to scale successfully. He needed people who not only had the right skills but also shared his vision, passion, and commitment to creating something extraordinary.

Recognizing the Need for Growth

It wasn't long before Alex began to notice the strain on his current team. The demands were growing faster than they could keep up with, and burnout started to rear its ugly head. Sarah, who had been with him since the early days, was still doing her best to manage the marketing efforts, but the increased complexity of the new features was requiring her to focus more on strategy than execution. Thomas was still the go-to guy for tech support and development, but his plate was becoming overwhelmingly full. As for Alex himself, he was doing everything he could to stay ahead of the growing demand, but he couldn't do it all.

The realization was sobering: if they were to continue their growth, they needed to expand their leadership team. The right hires could propel the business forward. But how could Alex find the right people?

Building the Core Team

Alex had learned a valuable lesson from the start-up phase of his business—growth wasn't just about the product, it was about building a culture and creating a team that worked together like a well-oiled machine. He needed leaders who could take responsibility and make decisions, so he could focus on strategic direction. But more than that, he needed to build a team that shared his vision of creating something genuinely impactful, not just another fitness app.

To begin, Alex sat down with Sarah and Thomas to discuss what roles they needed to fill. They had already recognized the need for a chief operating officer (COO) to help manage the day-to-day operations, someone who could handle the logistics and ensure that everything ran smoothly. Next, they needed a chief technology officer (CTO) who could drive the technical side of the business, overseeing the development of the coaching platform and ensuring the app could scale to meet the growing demand. And finally, they needed a head of customer experience—someone who could ensure that the personal coaching service was not just functional but deeply personalized and empathetic.

"We need leaders who can take the load off our shoulders," Alex said, after a long brainstorming session with Sarah and Thomas. "People who get the vision, who have the passion, but also the practical skills to keep everything running efficiently. The culture we've built is strong, but we need more hands to help steer the ship."

The Search Begins

The next few weeks were a whirlwind of interviews, calls, and networking events. Alex attended industry conferences, reached out to his network, and even posted job listings for key roles. It became clear that finding the right candidates wouldn't be easy. They needed individuals who were not only highly skilled but also aligned with the company's core values.

One of the first people to cross Alex's path was a woman named Claire, who had years of experience as a COO in the tech industry. She had helped scale several successful startups and had a no-nonsense approach to operations. Alex knew right away that she could bring the leadership and organizational skills that the business needed. She was a problem-solver and an excellent communicator—exactly what the company needed at this stage.

Next, Alex met with Ben, an experienced CTO who had worked for some of the biggest names in fitness tech. He had an impeccable technical background and a deep understanding of the industry. Ben's ability to think several steps ahead when it came to scalability and platform development impressed Alex. Ben also had a strong vision for how the personalized coaching experience could be improved even further with the right technological innovations.

Finally, Alex hired Maya, a seasoned expert in customer experience, who had worked for some of the leading brands in e-commerce. Maya's focus was on creating an empathetic, user-centric experience, and she understood how critical it was to make every customer feel valued. Her ability to build systems that made the coaching experience seamless and intuitive was exactly what the company needed.

Fostering a Collaborative Culture

Once Alex had built his core team, the next challenge was ensuring they worked together harmoniously. Alex had been used to being the decision-maker in the early days, but he knew that as the company grew, his role had to evolve. He needed to let go of some of the control and trust his team to make decisions. He had to create an environment where collaboration was not just encouraged but expected.

To build that culture, Alex set aside time every week for what he called "visionary meetings." These were sessions where the leadership team would discuss the long-term goals of the company and brainstorm ideas on how to stay ahead of the competition. The goal was to ensure that everyone was aligned, not just on the tasks at hand, but on the greater purpose of the company.

He also encouraged transparency. The team was empowered to share their ideas, concerns, and challenges openly. There were no "bad" ideas in these meetings—just discussions about how to create a better user experience, improve the product, and strengthen the company's values. As the team became more comfortable with each other, they began to gel, and the results spoke for themselves.

Leaning into Strengths

One of Alex's most important realizations during this time was the importance of leaning into the strengths of his team members. Claire, with her operational expertise, was able to streamline processes that had once been chaotic, allowing the team to scale without sacrificing quality. Ben, with his technical brilliance, spearheaded the development of new features that made the personalized coaching service even more effective, allowing for more granular tracking and deeper insights into user behavior. Maya worked tirelessly to improve customer engagement, ensuring that users not only felt supported but emotionally connected to their fitness journeys.

Each team member brought something vital to the table, and Alex knew that their combined efforts were what would ultimately push the business to new heights.

The Rewards of a Strong Team

As the months went on, the results of Alex's decision to build a strong team became evident. The business was growing faster than ever before, but more importantly, it was growing sustainably. New features were being rolled out consistently, customer feedback was overwhelmingly positive, and the personalized coaching experience was becoming the gold standard in the fitness industry.

Alex could finally step back and focus on what he did best—shaping the company's future and refining its strategic direction. He no longer had to worry about the day-to-day operations or the technical challenges; he had built a team he could trust to handle those tasks. With his leadership team in place, Alex could see the vision of his company coming to life in ways he hadn't imagined when he first started.

Lessons Learned

In reflecting on how far he had come, Alex realized that his journey had always been about people—whether it was his first customer, his loyal team, or his leadership group. Building a strong team wasn't just about finding the right skills—it was about finding individuals who were passionate, collaborative, and committed to the mission of the company.

He also learned that leadership was as much about trust as it was about decision-making. It was no longer about having all the answers; it was about empowering his team to succeed.

As the company grew and reached new milestones, Alex understood that success was never a solo journey. It was a collective effort, and the strength of his team was the backbone of the company's success.

The foundation had been built. The future was brighter than ever before.

Chapter 9: Scaling Up

With the core team in place and the business running smoothly, Alex faced the next great challenge: scaling. The company had reached a pivotal point where growth wasn't just about sustaining the existing model—it was about expanding to new markets, reaching more customers, and ensuring that the infrastructure could handle the increasing demands. The stakes were high, but Alex had learned through experience that scaling a business wasn't just a matter of increasing sales; it was about careful planning, investment, and smart decisions.

The Growing Pains

As Alex and his leadership team began discussing how to scale, it quickly became apparent that the initial strategies they had used in the early stages were no longer enough. The marketing campaigns that had worked so well in the past were starting to lose their impact, and customer demand was growing at a rate that was difficult to predict. The company was at a crossroads—if they didn't scale properly, they could easily lose control of the operations they had worked so hard to build.

The first major challenge was infrastructure. Their tech platform, which had been able to handle a smaller user base, was beginning to show signs of strain. The app was slow at times, and customer support inquiries were piling up. Alex could see that they needed to improve their technical infrastructure to handle a larger volume of users without sacrificing the quality of service that had been key to their success.

He called a meeting with Ben, their CTO, to discuss the technical roadmap for scaling.

"We need to upgrade the platform," Alex said. "The demand is only going to increase, and if we don't get ahead of it, we'll lose customers. We can't afford to fall behind."

Ben nodded, looking through the current system's performance metrics. "Agreed. We need to transition to a more scalable cloud solution, and I think we should also consider investing in AI to enhance personalization and optimize user engagement. But it's going to take time and money."

Investing in Technology and Innovation

With the decision to overhaul their tech infrastructure in motion, Alex turned his attention to another critical area—marketing. While their organic growth had been impressive, they needed to accelerate their customer acquisition to match the scale of their operations. But how?

Maya, the head of customer experience, had been researching new ways to enhance engagement with their user base. "We've built strong loyalty, but now it's about expanding reach," she said during a strategy meeting. "We need to target different demographics and leverage partnerships with influencers, health bloggers, and fitness experts who can showcase the value of personalized coaching."

To achieve this, Alex made the decision to allocate more resources to paid marketing, including social media campaigns, influencer partnerships, and targeted ads. They would also develop more engaging content—blog posts, videos, and webinars that demonstrated the effectiveness of their personalized coaching and fostered a sense of community.

But scaling was about more than just attracting new customers. It was about optimizing the current processes and systems to handle the increase in demand. Alex, along with Claire, the COO, identified the need to streamline operations even further. They needed a stronger supply chain, better training for the growing customer support team, and improved automation tools to reduce manual tasks.

The Expansion Challenge

As the business continued to grow, Alex knew it wasn't just enough to scale within their current market. He had always believed in the power of global reach, and now was the time to take that leap. He wanted to take the company beyond the borders of their home country and make the product available internationally.

The team researched potential markets, focusing on regions where personalized fitness coaching would resonate, especially where the fitness culture was growing. Alex was particularly interested in entering the European and Southeast Asian markets. But international expansion came with its own set of challenges—local regulations, cultural differences, and the need to adapt the product to different languages and customs.

"We need to localize the experience for these new markets," Ben said, pointing to a map of their target regions. "From the content to the app itself, everything needs to feel familiar to the user, no matter where they are."

That meant hiring local teams for customer support, marketing, and partnerships. They would need to tailor the marketing materials to each region's unique audience, develop region-specific fitness content, and even offer customer support in different languages. Additionally, Alex would need to navigate the complexities of international business law and adapt their pricing models to reflect the local economies.

Capital and Funding

As Alex's vision of scaling the business took shape, one of the most pressing concerns was funding. Scaling at this level would require significant capital to support the tech upgrades, the international expansion, and the increased marketing spend. Alex knew he would have to seek out investors who shared his vision for the company's future.

He reached out to several venture capital firms, pitching his story and the company's potential. The growth they had seen in the past year was impressive, but the real opportunity lay in the company's ability to scale globally. After a series of meetings and negotiations, Alex secured the funding he needed to fuel the next stage of expansion. The capital infusion gave the company the breathing room it needed to accelerate their plans without sacrificing quality or service.

Delegating and Trusting the Team

With the business growing and the pressure mounting, Alex realized that he could no longer manage every aspect of the company. He had learned early on that building a successful business was about assembling the right team, but now he had to take that one step further—he had to delegate authority. This wasn't easy for Alex, as he had always prided himself on being hands-on and deeply involved in every decision.

However, the more the business expanded, the more he had to trust the leadership team. Claire was already overseeing day-to-day operations and ensuring that the systems were running smoothly. Ben was leading the technical improvements and development of new features. Maya was spearheading marketing campaigns and customer experience initiatives. With each team member stepping up and taking on more responsibility, Alex found that he could focus on long-term strategy and vision.

The key to scaling wasn't just in the systems and infrastructure—it was in the people. Alex realized that the company's growth was a direct result of the collective effort of the team. He wasn't doing it alone anymore, and that made all the difference.

The Results of Scaling Up

As the months passed, the changes began to show. The upgraded tech platform was running smoothly, handling an increasing number of users without issues. Marketing efforts were paying off, and new customer acquisition was higher than ever. The company had expanded into multiple international markets, with localized versions of the app and customer support in key languages. Revenue was growing exponentially, and customer feedback was overwhelmingly positive.

Alex couldn't help but reflect on how far they had come. Just a year ago, the business had been struggling to break even. Now, it was a global enterprise with a dedicated and passionate team behind it. But as much as Alex celebrated the milestones, he knew that scaling wasn't the end—it was just another beginning.

Lessons Learned

Scaling up had been one of the most challenging but rewarding experiences of Alex's career. The key takeaways were clear:

1. **Technology is Essential:** A scalable infrastructure is the backbone of growth. Without the right tech stack, everything else falls apart.

2. **Global Vision, Local Execution:** When expanding internationally, it's essential to adapt the product and marketing to local cultures while staying true to the core values.
3. **Delegate and Trust:** The more you scale, the less you can do on your own. A strong team is key to ensuring growth remains sustainable.
4. **Smart Funding:** Scaling requires capital, but it's important to align with investors who share your vision for long-term growth.

As Alex stood at the helm of his growing business, he understood that scaling was not a one-time event—it was an ongoing process of adapting, innovating, and refining. The future looked brighter than ever, but Alex knew that the key to success was not just about growing bigger—it was about growing smarter. The next chapter of the company's journey was just beginning, and he was ready to lead it into the future.

Part 4: The Impact

Chapter 10: The Ethical Dilemma

As Alex's business grew into a formidable force in the market, success seemed inevitable. The company was thriving—revenue was soaring, customer satisfaction was high, and the global expansion was going according to plan. Yet, with every step forward, Alex couldn't shake the feeling that the larger his business became, the more complicated the decisions. What had once been a small operation grounded in idealistic principles now had to navigate a minefield of ethical dilemmas.

A New Opportunity

One afternoon, while Alex was sitting in his office reviewing financial reports, he received a call from Carl, one of the company's largest investors. Carl had always been supportive, offering not only capital but also valuable strategic advice. But today, Carl sounded different—his tone was measured, almost cautious.

"Alex," Carl began, "I have a new opportunity for you. A company in the health tech space is looking for a buyer. They're in a bit of a financial crunch, but their technology could be a game changer for us. It's proprietary, and it's advanced—something that would propel us ahead of the competition."

Alex paused, his interest piqued. He had always been open to new opportunities, especially ones that could expand their product offerings. The company had been looking to enhance its app with advanced features that incorporated biometric data and AI-driven recommendations for its users. This acquisition could be just the solution.

"Sounds interesting," Alex replied. "But why are they selling? And is there any risk?"

Carl hesitated. "They've been struggling with some internal issues, mainly around data privacy concerns. There's a lawsuit pending, and they've been accused of misusing customer data. But that's not our problem, right? We can clean up their mess and take their tech."

Alex's stomach dropped slightly. He had heard of the company in question and knew the controversy surrounding them. The lawsuit involved allegations that they had mishandled sensitive health data, potentially exposing customer information. Even though they were still operational, the company's reputation had been tarnished. Taking on their technology would mean inheriting their liabilities, but Carl's confidence in the deal made Alex question whether it was a risk worth taking.

The Dilemma of Ethics

That night, as Alex lay in bed, he replayed the conversation over and over in his mind. On one hand, the acquisition of this new technology could solidify their position in the market. It would be a game-changer, and in the cutthroat world of business, it would give them a huge competitive edge. On the other hand, Alex couldn't ignore the ethical implications. Would it be right to take over a company with such a problematic history, especially when it involved sensitive customer data?

He knew that privacy was a cornerstone of the business's values. From the very beginning, Alex had promised customers that their data would be treated with the utmost respect. To use the technology of a company that had violated that trust felt like a betrayal of the very foundation upon which he had built his brand.

The ethical dilemma weighed heavily on Alex. He wasn't the kind of leader who ignored morals for the sake of profit. He understood the power of a strong reputation, and he knew that customers valued transparency and trust more than anything. But could he afford to pass up an opportunity that could secure the future of the business? Was he willing to risk falling behind in the race to stay competitive, or was this a time when his values had to take precedence?

Consulting the Team

The next morning, Alex gathered his leadership team to discuss the potential acquisition. He didn't want to make this decision alone; he needed their input. Everyone had a different perspective on the matter, and he knew it would be important to consider all viewpoints before moving forward.

Claire, the COO, was the first to speak. "It's a great opportunity in terms of growth, Alex. But we need to think about how it might impact the public perception of our company. If we buy this company and there's a scandal, our reputation could suffer."

Maya, the head of customer experience, nodded in agreement. "Trust is everything in this industry. If our users find out that we've acquired a company with questionable data practices, we risk alienating them. Even if we clean up the mess, it will take years to rebuild that trust."

Ben, the CTO, was more pragmatic. "Technologically, the acquisition makes sense. The AI and biometric features could drastically improve the app and set us apart from our competitors. But I agree with Claire and Maya—it's a fine line. We'd need to invest heavily in improving their infrastructure and security protocols to ensure we're not inheriting their liabilities."

Alex listened to his team's concerns, and for the first time in a long time, he felt unsure. The acquisition represented growth and progress, but it also came with a moral price. His team had given him their honest opinions, and now he had to make the final call.

The Decision

For the next few days, Alex did nothing but reflect. He spent long hours revisiting the company's mission statement, reading through the core values that had guided him since the early days. At the heart of it all, Alex realized, was a commitment to integrity. No matter how many customers they gained or how much revenue they earned, if the business lost its moral compass, it would all be for nothing.

On the fourth day after the meeting, Alex made the decision. He called Carl to inform him that they would not be moving forward with the acquisition. It was a difficult decision to make, especially knowing the opportunity they were passing up. But deep down, Alex knew it was the right one.

The Ripple Effect

After informing Carl, Alex met with his team to discuss the decision. At first, some of them were disappointed. They had all recognized the potential of the technology and the business boost it could provide. But as they discussed the matter further, they began to understand the bigger picture.

Claire, who had initially been the most vocal against the acquisition, was the first to speak up. "I think you made the right call, Alex. We can't sacrifice what we stand for, especially not for a short-term gain."

Maya agreed, adding, "Our customers trust us to protect their information. If we took on a company with a tarnished reputation, it would be hard to regain that trust. We're doing the right thing by putting ethics before profits."

Ben, too, acknowledged the wisdom in Alex's decision. "I've seen how a lack of ethics can destroy a business, even the most successful ones. We'll find other ways to innovate. We don't need to compromise our values to stay ahead."

The team rallied behind Alex's decision. They knew that, in the long run, staying true to their mission would yield greater rewards than any technology acquisition ever could.

The Moral of the Story

Alex's decision to pass on the acquisition of the controversial company was a defining moment in his journey as a business leader. The lesson he learned was simple yet profound: success in business isn't just about financial growth or market share—it's about staying true to your values and maintaining integrity, no matter the cost. While the temptation of quick success can be strong, it's the long-term reputation of your business that ultimately determines your success.

The ethical dilemma Alex faced was a reminder that every business decision, big or small, has far-reaching consequences. In the end, the company's success was not defined by the technologies it acquired or the deals it struck—it was defined by the trust it built with its customers and the commitment it made to never compromise its integrity.

Chapter 11: The Crisis

No business, no matter how successful, is immune to challenges. It's easy to celebrate victories, but it's the ability to endure crises that truly defines a company's resilience. For Alex, his company's true test was about to begin.

The Unexpected Storm

It started with a call early on a Tuesday morning—a call that would forever change the trajectory of the business. Alex's phone rang, the caller ID displaying an unfamiliar number. It was Sam, the lead developer from the tech department.

"Alex, we've got a serious issue," Sam said, his voice tense. "It's the app. There's been a breach."

Alex's stomach dropped. "What do you mean, 'a breach'?"

"It looks like someone has accessed user accounts, and it's not just a couple of them. It's thousands. We're talking about sensitive data—personal information, payment details... everything. We're tracking the breach now, but it's spreading fast."

Alex felt his heart race. This was every entrepreneur's worst nightmare. A data breach could ruin everything—the company's reputation, its hard-earned trust, and its future.

"Sam, how did this happen?" Alex asked, trying to stay calm.

"We're still investigating, but it looks like a vulnerability in one of the recent updates. We didn't catch it in testing. We're working on containing it, but we need your direction, fast."

Alex took a deep breath, pushing away the rising panic. "I'll be there in twenty minutes. Keep me updated."

The Initial Panic

As Alex arrived at the office, the gravity of the situation became more apparent. The room was filled with the tech team, heads down, scrambling to figure out how the breach had happened and, more importantly, how to stop it. The usual sense of controlled chaos had taken a darker turn. Everyone was on edge, typing furiously on their laptops, making calls to security experts, and reviewing data logs.

Claire, the COO, greeted him with a grim expression. "Alex, it's bad. We've already notified the authorities, and we're working with cybersecurity firms to contain the breach. But we need a public statement ready. The longer we wait, the worse this is going to look."

"Do we know who's responsible?" Alex asked.

"Not yet. But we'll find out. For now, we need to secure the system and stop the leak."

Maya, who had joined the meeting, was visibly shaken. "The worst part is the trust factor. People are going to want answers. They're going to want to know how we let this happen."

Alex nodded. He knew she was right. Trust, the very cornerstone of their business, was now on the line. If they didn't act quickly, customers would abandon them, and competitors would seize the opportunity to pounce.

Facing the Fallout

Within hours, the news spread like wildfire. Social media exploded with complaints, and reports of the breach began to surface on news sites. People were furious. Some were calling for a boycott of the company, while others demanded full transparency about what had happened. A sense of panic settled over the team. The storm had arrived, and it was relentless.

Alex knew that the company had to act fast. They couldn't afford to hide from the truth; they had to face the crisis head-on. He called an emergency meeting with his leadership team. The focus was clear: damage control.

"We need to release a statement immediately," Claire suggested. "Acknowledge the breach, explain what we're doing to fix it, and reassure our users that we're doing everything we can to protect their data moving forward."

Maya agreed, adding, "Transparency is key. We can't afford to downplay this. If we try to hide anything, we'll lose even more trust."

Alex understood. They had to own the mistake and show their commitment to correcting it. He drafted a statement with the communications team, detailing the breach, the steps being taken to mitigate the damage, and offering affected users a year of free credit monitoring.

But as the hours turned into days, the crisis only seemed to deepen. The media reports became more sensational, with some outlets speculating on the severity of the breach and hinting at insider involvement. The company's stock price plummeted, and several major investors started pulling out.

It was becoming clear that this wasn't just a technical issue—it was a public relations disaster.

The Pressure Mounts

As the days wore on, Alex's stress levels reached an all-time high. He spent sleepless nights poring over reports, meeting with cybersecurity firms, and communicating with key stakeholders. But no matter how much effort he put into handling the crisis, the fallout kept growing. The pressure was relentless, and he could feel the weight of the world bearing down on him.

It wasn't just the company that was at risk—it was his personal reputation. For years, Alex had prided himself on building a business grounded in trust, transparency, and integrity. He had worked hard to create a brand that customers believed in. Now, it felt like everything he had worked for was unraveling in front of his eyes.

The team was feeling the strain as well. Claire was more distant than usual, and Maya seemed overwhelmed, though she remained committed to doing everything she could to salvage the company's image. Ben, the CTO, who had always been the calm, collected problem-solver, was visibly anxious, constantly in meetings with the tech team trying to patch the vulnerabilities and prevent further breaches.

The Wake-Up Call

One evening, after yet another long day of crisis management, Alex found himself alone in his office. The weight of the situation hit him like a ton of bricks. His head ached, his thoughts were jumbled, and he couldn't remember the last time he had eaten properly.

But as he sat there, staring at the glowing screen of his laptop, he was struck by a realization. He wasn't the only one affected by this crisis. His employees, his customers, even his family—they were all dealing with the fallout of this breach.

In that moment, Alex understood something critical. The crisis wasn't just about the business; it was about the people who had supported him along the way. They were all in this together, and it wasn't just his company on the line—it was their collective future. He had to fight for them.

Determined, Alex made a decision. He couldn't let this crisis break him. He had to lead his team through this, show them that failure wasn't an option. But more than that, he had to prove that even in the darkest moments, a true leader stands firm.

Turning the Tide

The next morning, Alex gathered his team for a meeting. His resolve was clear.

"We're going to fix this," he said, his voice steady. "We've faced challenges before, and we'll face this one too. But it's going to take all of us. We're going to show our customers that we're taking responsibility, and we're going to make things right. This isn't just about fixing a technical issue; it's about showing the world who we are as a company. We will come out of this stronger, together."

The team rallied around him. They worked tirelessly, addressing every concern, communicating openly with their customers, and offering solutions. Slowly, the tide began to turn. The media reports became more balanced, focusing on the company's efforts to recover and rebuild. Customers appreciated the transparency, and while there were still complaints, many were supportive of the company's dedication to fixing the problem.

The Long Road Ahead

It took months, but the crisis eventually passed. The breach was contained, the affected customers were compensated, and the company began to recover its reputation. It wasn't easy, and it wasn't quick, but Alex had learned something invaluable: in times of crisis, a leader's true strength is revealed not by how they handle success, but by how they rise from the ashes of failure.

The company emerged from the crisis stronger, more resilient, and more committed than ever to its core values. Alex knew the road ahead would still have its challenges, but he was ready for whatever came next. He had faced the storm, and not only had he survived—it had made him a better leader.

Chapter 12: The Expansion

When Alex's company began to recover from the crisis, he realized something important: their journey wasn't over. In fact, it was only just beginning. The storm of the data breach had passed, but now he had to refocus his efforts on scaling the business, expanding its reach, and solidifying the foundation for long-term success.

The lessons learned during the crisis had made him stronger. His leadership, the trust he had earned from his team, and the newfound resilience of the company all pointed toward a bright future—if they could seize the opportunity to expand.

The Vision of Growth

Alex sat in his office late one night, a whiteboard full of scribbles and charts glowing under the dim lights. The company had survived its worst crisis, but what now? The business had rebounded, but it wasn't enough. Alex knew that if they were to achieve sustainable success, they needed to expand beyond their current borders.

"Expansion is the next logical step," Alex muttered to himself, as he stared at the numbers. He remembered the advice from his first mentor, Thomas, who had said that true growth meant stepping outside of your comfort zone, even when things were uncertain.

The problem was that the company had already proven its worth in their initial market, but now they had to look beyond their established customer base. It was time to venture into new territories, new products, and possibly even new markets. But it wasn't going to be easy. Expansion would come with new risks, and Alex had learned through experience that rushing into things could lead to disaster.

He made a decision: it was time to bring in the right people. He needed experienced minds, advisors who had navigated the complex terrain of business expansion before.

Seeking Expertise

Alex reached out to several industry experts, people he trusted and respected. One of them was a seasoned entrepreneur named Rachel, who had built and sold multiple businesses in the tech space. She had gone through the grind of scaling a company, navigating competitive markets, and dealing with the logistical nightmare of expanding internationally.

Rachel agreed to meet with Alex at his office. Over lunch, they discussed the intricacies of scaling a business—everything from financial management to operational efficiency, to understanding the legal challenges of operating in new regions.

"You've done well with your core market," Rachel said, leaning forward, "but now you need to look at infrastructure. Your team, your technology, and most importantly, your customer experience. Expansion isn't just about reaching more people—it's about doing so while maintaining the same quality and trust that you built your reputation on."

Alex took mental notes, his mind buzzing with possibilities. Rachel's words hit home. Expansion wasn't just about financials and growth rates—it was about maintaining the integrity of what they had built while taking on new challenges.

The Global Reach

The idea of going global had always lingered in Alex's mind. He knew that the digital age made it possible to access customers worldwide, but he also knew that geographical expansion required meticulous planning. It wasn't just about translating a website into different languages and launching in new regions—it was about understanding the cultural nuances, customer behavior, and business regulations of those countries.

With Rachel's advice, Alex began by conducting market research in several countries where they had identified potential growth. They needed to understand customer needs and how their product could meet those needs in ways that were relevant to local cultures.

They started small—testing the waters in a few select countries with a localized version of their product. Alex hired a team of experts to conduct user testing, focus groups, and surveys, making sure that their products and services were aligned with local preferences. They also adjusted their marketing strategies to fit the social norms and values of each region, focusing on authenticity and relevance.

The Financial Leap

The next hurdle was financing their expansion. They needed capital—more than ever before. Alex knew that to expand, they would have to invest heavily in technology, operations, and marketing. He reached out to investors who had supported him in the past, but he also knew that this time, they would need more than just a pitch. They needed a concrete plan that demonstrated how the expansion would bring long-term value to the company.

Alex worked closely with Claire, who was now handling investor relations, to refine the pitch.

They made sure to address the risks involved while emphasizing the potential for growth in international markets. They were transparent about the lessons they had learned from the past, and how they would apply those lessons to ensure they didn't repeat the mistakes they had made during the early stages of the company.

With a solid plan in place, they secured the funding they needed. But even with the financial backing, Alex knew that success would depend on how well they could execute their strategy.

Building a Global Infrastructure

The next step in their expansion was building the infrastructure to support their growth. Alex and his team had already begun expanding their headquarters, but now they needed to create a network of support offices, local partnerships, and logistics hubs around the world.

"We can't just rely on one office anymore," Claire said. "We need to build relationships in every country we're entering, from local suppliers to customer service teams. Every touchpoint with the customer has to be seamless, and that means having boots on the ground in each region."

Alex agreed. They hired local managers who were familiar with the intricacies of business in their regions, ensuring that they could effectively adapt to the local market. They also invested in scalable technology systems that would allow them to track customer data, manage inventory, and monitor performance from a centralized location.

The Risk of Overstretching

As they expanded further, Alex found himself facing a new challenge: the risk of overstretching the company's resources. It wasn't just about taking on more business—it was about managing growth without compromising quality.

In a meeting with Rachel, Alex expressed his concerns. "I'm worried that we might be taking on too much. We're growing rapidly, but I don't want to lose sight of the things that made us successful in the first place."

Rachel nodded. "That's the biggest risk of expansion—getting caught up in the excitement of growth and forgetting about the fundamentals. You have to keep one eye on the big picture, but the other has to stay on your core values. If you lose sight of what makes your company unique, the expansion will become a liability, not an opportunity."

Alex took her words to heart. They made strategic decisions to slow down their expansion and focus on strengthening the infrastructure they had already built. They didn't just want to grow—they wanted to grow sustainably.

New Challenges and New Opportunities

As they moved into new territories, they began to see the positive effects of their careful planning. The company's international reach was growing, and with it came new opportunities. They secured partnerships with major distributors, negotiated exclusive deals with local retailers, and began to see their brand recognized globally.

But there were still challenges to face. Regulatory hurdles, cultural differences, and the complexity of global competition were constant concerns. Yet, Alex was confident that the lessons learned in the past—the crisis, the failures, and the hard-earned successes—had prepared him for this moment.

He had learned that true growth wasn't just about expanding your footprint. It was about evolving into a stronger, more resilient company, capable of weathering any storm. And with that mindset, Alex was ready to lead his company into the future.

Part 5: Legacy

Chapter 13: Giving Back

As Alex looked out of his office window one afternoon, he couldn't help but reflect on the incredible journey his company had taken over the years. From humble beginnings to global expansion, from countless failures to groundbreaking successes, he had come a long way. His business had reached a level he had once only dreamed of, and yet, despite all the accolades, something was missing. Alex had always believed in the power of giving back, and as the company grew, so did his desire to contribute to causes that mattered.

It had been a constant theme throughout his life: helping others. He had been fortunate enough to have mentors, family, and friends who supported him during his struggles. Now, it was his turn to extend a hand to those in need.

The Idea of Giving

The idea of corporate social responsibility (CSR) had been something Alex had pondered for a while. For many successful entrepreneurs, the transition from focusing solely on business success to making a tangible social impact was a defining moment. Alex wanted to ensure that his company's success would not just be measured by its profits, but also by the positive change it could create in the world.

He sat down with his team to discuss the possibilities. As they brainstormed, the conversation quickly shifted from charitable donations to something much more ambitious. Alex didn't just want to give money away—he wanted to create a program that would make a real difference, something sustainable that could impact people's lives for years to come.

After several meetings, they came up with an idea: The "Future Leaders Initiative." The program would focus on helping underserved communities by providing scholarships, mentorship, and job placement assistance to young people. It wasn't just about financial aid—it was about empowering the next generation of entrepreneurs, leaders, and change-makers.

The Future Leaders Initiative

The idea behind the "Future Leaders Initiative" was simple but powerful: offer educational support and mentorship to individuals who otherwise wouldn't have the opportunity to access higher education or start their own businesses. Alex and his team would collaborate with local schools, universities, and non-profits to identify young people with potential but lacking the resources to reach their full potential. The program would offer them scholarships, internships, and career coaching, as well as hands-on experience working within Alex's company.

But Alex knew that this initiative would need more than just financial backing. It would require a long-term commitment from his company to make it sustainable. He tasked his HR department with organizing a team of mentors, including successful leaders from various industries who could provide guidance to these young people. It would take time, but Alex was ready to make the investment.

First Steps in Giving Back

The program kicked off in their home city, with Alex personally visiting local schools and community centers to introduce the initiative. The response was overwhelming. Schools were eager to partner, and many students expressed interest in applying for scholarships and mentorship opportunities. Alex felt an intense sense of fulfillment as he saw how excited and motivated these young people were. Their dreams, much like his own once were, were vast—filled with hopes of starting businesses, creating jobs, and making an impact.

One of the first applicants, a young woman named Maria, stood out to Alex. She had grown up in a low-income neighborhood, raised by a single mother who worked multiple jobs to support her family. Despite the challenges, Maria had excelled in school and had aspirations of becoming a tech entrepreneur. However, the lack of resources and opportunities made it almost impossible for her to realize her dreams.

Maria applied for the program, and after several rounds of interviews and assessments, she was selected as one of the first scholarship recipients. Alex personally met her during the announcement, and her eyes lit up with disbelief and joy.

"This is going to change my life," she said, tears welling up in her eyes. "I didn't think someone like me would ever get a chance like this."

Alex smiled, understanding that this was the essence of what the program was about. It wasn't just about financial aid—it was about opening doors, giving people the resources, and most importantly, the belief that they could achieve their dreams.

Empowering Others

Over the next few years, the Future Leaders Initiative began to grow. More and more young people joined the program, and the impact became undeniable. Students graduated from top universities, landed their first jobs, and in many cases, even started their own businesses. Alex's company provided internships and job placements, ensuring that these young talents would have a platform to grow.

Maria was one of the first success stories. After completing her studies, she was offered a full-time position at a tech firm, and not long after, she launched her own start-up in the technology space. Maria's story was a testament to the power of mentorship and opportunity, and it inspired many others to take the leap into entrepreneurship.

Alex had set out to give back, but what he found was that in doing so, he had created a ripple effect—one that had far-reaching consequences. As more individuals succeeded through the program, they, in turn, gave back to their communities, creating a culture of generosity and support that spread far beyond what Alex had initially imagined.

The Impact of Giving

The impact of the Future Leaders Initiative was profound. Not only had Alex's company helped to create new opportunities for young people, but it had also shifted the company culture itself.

The employees who had volunteered as mentors found deep fulfillment in helping others. It brought the team closer together, reminded them of the values that had driven their own success, and reignited their passion for the work they were doing.

The initiative also earned recognition in the media, and Alex was invited to speak at conferences about the importance of giving back as part of a company's long-term strategy. His story was one of resilience, but also of compassion and responsibility. As Alex stood on stage, addressing a room full of entrepreneurs and business leaders, he knew that this was the moment he had been waiting for.

"This," he said, looking out at the audience, "is the true measure of success. It's not just about the profits we make. It's about the people we help, the lives we change, and the legacy we leave behind."

The Life-Changing Moral

As the years went by, Alex came to realize something profound: true success was not measured in revenue, market share, or accolades—it was measured by the positive change you brought into the world. Giving back wasn't just a way to make the world a better place; it was a way to create a life full of purpose.

Through the Future Leaders Initiative, Alex had given countless young people the opportunity to achieve their dreams, just as he had been given that same chance early in his life. But more than that, Alex had learned the most important lesson of all: success wasn't about what you accumulated—it was about what you shared with others.

Alex's business had flourished, but it was his commitment to giving back that had made him a true success. In helping others achieve their dreams, Alex had found a fulfillment that no business deal or financial triumph could ever provide.

And so, as he looked out over his growing empire, Alex smiled with the knowledge that he had not only built a thriving company but had also created a legacy that would inspire and empower others for generations to come.

Chapter 14: The Full Circle

Years had passed since Alex first started his entrepreneurial journey. His company had grown into a global powerhouse, and the Future Leaders Initiative had become a legacy that would endure far beyond his time. But despite all the success, accolades, and recognition, Alex knew that there was still one final chapter to write in his story.

He had come full circle—back to where it all began.

Reflection

It was an early morning when Alex sat alone in his office, staring at the city skyline through the floor-to-ceiling windows. The office had changed over the years. The once humble space had been replaced with a sophisticated, sleek design that reflected the magnitude of the company's success. Yet, for all the grand changes, something felt deeply familiar—almost nostalgic.

The world had changed. His company had changed. Alex had changed. But as he reflected on the path that had brought him here, he couldn't help but remember the challenges and doubts that had plagued him early on. Those sleepless nights in his tiny apartment, the late hours spent brainstorming with friends, the painful failures, and the moments of triumph—they all led to this point.

The journey had been long, but it had been worth it.

Returning to the Roots

Over the past few years, Alex had spent more time mentoring the next generation of entrepreneurs through the Future Leaders Initiative. He had seen countless young minds grow, flourish, and venture out into the world with new ideas and unshakeable confidence. He had helped them shape their futures, but now, something was calling him to give back in a more personal way.

It was a feeling he had been grappling with for some time. As much as he enjoyed running the company, as much as he appreciated the luxury and comfort that came with his success, Alex realized there was something deeper, something more fulfilling he wanted to pursue. He had always known that success wasn't just about business—it was about creating a meaningful life. And now, after years of building, leading, and guiding others, Alex felt the urge to return to his roots.

He thought about the struggles he'd faced in his early days, and how much he had been helped by the few key individuals who had mentored him along the way. He thought about the lessons he had learned, not just from books or business practices, but from the people who had shaped his character. His mentor, Steve, who had taught him resilience; his business partner, Maria, who had shown him the value of trust; and his parents, whose unwavering support had been the bedrock of his determination.

Alex realized that now, it was his turn to help others in a more profound way—not just through the business or the program, but by stepping out of his comfort zone and giving back directly, one-on-one, to those who needed it most.

The New Mission

It started with a call to Steve. Steve, now retired and enjoying a quiet life, had been a father figure to Alex for many years. Alex explained to him how he felt the need to return to his roots, to start a new project that would allow him to work directly with the next wave of entrepreneurs, those who had the passion but lacked the resources or guidance.

"Steve, I've been thinking about this for a while," Alex said, his voice tinged with excitement. "I want to start something new—something more personal. I'm not talking about a company. I'm talking about a foundation. A place where people can come, learn, and grow with real-world guidance from those who've been there."

Steve listened intently, and after a long pause, he replied, "I always knew you were going to do something big, Alex. You've got the heart for it. I'm in."

With Steve's support, Alex began working on what would soon become "The Full Circle Foundation." The mission was clear: to provide hands-on mentorship, training, and support to aspiring entrepreneurs in underserved communities, focusing on the social impact aspect of business. The foundation would not just be about creating successful entrepreneurs; it would be about fostering a sense of community, responsibility, and giving back.

The Full Circle Foundation would operate differently from the Future Leaders Initiative. Instead of offering scholarships and job placements, it would offer a more immersive experience. Entrepreneurs would spend time with seasoned mentors, gaining practical experience while learning the ins and outs of business from the ground up. The foundation would emphasize the importance of ethical leadership, social entrepreneurship, and long-term vision.

Alex knew that this wouldn't be easy. The foundation's goals were ambitious. But it felt like the right next step. The foundation would be an extension of his belief that business success could go hand-in-hand with making the world a better place.

The First Entrepreneur

The Full Circle Foundation's first mentee was a young woman named Lara. She had come from a small town where opportunities were scarce. Lara had always been passionate about sustainable fashion, and her dream was to launch a brand that would change the way people thought about clothing. But she didn't have the financial backing, nor did she know where to start.

Alex met Lara during a pitch session at the foundation. She stood before him, nervous but determined, explaining her vision for an eco-friendly clothing line. Alex saw a spark in her—raw potential, but also a lack of direction. He decided to take her under his wing, not just as a mentor, but as someone who would help her shape her vision into a reality.

Lara's journey at the foundation was transformative. She learned everything from sourcing sustainable materials to creating a business plan, to marketing and building a loyal customer base. Alex, Steve, and other mentors worked with her every step of the way, offering advice, connections, and a wealth of knowledge. It wasn't easy, and there were moments of doubt. But with Alex's guidance, Lara's brand took shape.

Months later, she launched her first collection. The response was overwhelming. Not just for the quality of the clothing, but for the story behind the brand—how it was built on the principles of sustainability, ethical practices, and a desire to make a difference.

Lara's success was a testament to the power of mentorship and community, and it reinforced Alex's belief that business could be a force for good.

The Ripple Effect

As more entrepreneurs came through the foundation, Alex watched as the ripple effect of mentorship began to grow. The businesses that emerged weren't just financially successful—they were socially responsible, rooted in values that Alex had always held dear. His approach to business had come full circle: it wasn't just about the financial gain or the recognition—it was about creating opportunities, empowering others, and making a lasting impact on the world.

The Full Circle Foundation became a thriving hub for aspiring entrepreneurs, offering resources, networking, and guidance. Over time, it expanded to include workshops, leadership development programs, and even venture capital opportunities for those with the drive and ideas to change the world.

Alex's company continued to thrive, but he had found something more meaningful in the foundation. It had become a place of personal fulfillment, where he could give back in a way that went beyond just financial contributions. The foundation was his legacy—a way for him to ensure that the principles of integrity, community, and ethical business practices would continue to guide the next generation of leaders.

The Final Lesson

As Alex stood in front of the group of new entrepreneurs at the Full Circle Foundation's annual event, he could feel the sense of pride swelling in his chest. These young entrepreneurs, each with their own dreams, challenges, and visions, were the future of business. And Alex knew that by giving them the tools, knowledge, and support they needed, he was not just changing their lives—he was changing the world.

He paused, looking at the faces in the room, and then spoke.

"When I started this journey, I was just a kid with a dream," Alex began. "I had no idea what the future held, and I faced so many obstacles along the way. But the one thing that kept me going was the belief that success is not just about what you build—it's about what you give back. This foundation is proof that when you lift others up, when you help them realize their potential, you create a ripple effect that lasts far beyond your own lifetime. Remember, the true measure of success is not the business you build, but the lives you touch along the way."

Chapter 15: The Legacy Continues

The sun was setting on another successful year at the Full Circle Foundation. The headquarters, now a state-of-the-art building in the heart of the city, had grown over the years to accommodate the increasing number of young entrepreneurs seeking guidance. As Alex sat in his office, looking out over the bustling city below, he reflected on how far the foundation had come. But it wasn't just about the physical space or the recognition—it was about the legacy they were building together.

For Alex, the foundation had become something far more significant than he could have ever imagined. It was his legacy, and it was clear to him now that the real work was just beginning.

A New Generation of Leaders

In recent months, Alex had noticed something remarkable. The entrepreneurs who had once entered the Full Circle Foundation as aspiring dreamers were now beginning to lead their own initiatives, paying forward the mentorship and lessons they had received. This was the ripple effect Alex had always hoped for—a new generation of leaders who would continue the work of the foundation and inspire others to do the same.

One of the most notable examples was Lara, the young woman who had launched her sustainable fashion line years ago. Now, she had expanded her business into a global brand and had also started her own mentorship program within the Full Circle Foundation. Her success story had become one of many that highlighted the transformative power of guidance, persistence, and giving back.

But Lara was just one example. Dozens of others were following in her footsteps, each with their own unique contributions to their industries. The impact was growing, and Alex knew that the foundation's work was having a lasting effect on the world.

The Future of Full Circle

The success of the Full Circle Foundation was evident, but Alex was a visionary. He knew that the work they had started needed to grow even further, reaching more people and creating a broader impact. He envisioned a network of entrepreneurial hubs spanning the globe, with local centers in underserved communities, where aspiring leaders could access the tools, education, and mentorship they needed to thrive.

To achieve this, Alex began discussing partnerships with influential organizations, universities, and investors who shared his vision for social entrepreneurship. He reached out to former mentees who had found success and asked them to join him in expanding the foundation's reach, offering their expertise and support to new generations of entrepreneurs. He envisioned a collaborative effort, where the foundation didn't just give back to individuals but to entire communities, helping them build sustainable economies and drive social change.

The idea was bold, but Alex was used to bold ideas by now. He believed that the world was ready for a shift—one where business and social responsibility went hand in hand, where success was measured not by profits alone, but by the number of lives transformed and the positive changes made in the world.

Passing the Torch

As the years went on, Alex's role in the foundation gradually evolved. He was still actively involved, but his focus shifted from day-to-day operations to overseeing the broader vision. He began to see the new leaders within the foundation as the torchbearers of its mission.

It was during a special event, the 10th anniversary celebration of the Full Circle Foundation, that Alex realized just how much his legacy had already taken root. A ceremony was held, where several alumni of the foundation were recognized for their extraordinary contributions to their fields and communities. Each story told was a testament to the power of mentorship and the principles Alex had instilled in them.

Standing at the front of the room, Lara, now a seasoned entrepreneur and mentor, spoke to the crowd. "I'm standing here today because someone believed in me when I didn't believe in myself. Alex was more than just a mentor—he became family, a guide who showed me the path to my dreams. And now, it's my turn to pass that belief on to others."

Alex watched with pride as Lara finished her speech, and his heart swelled with emotion. The legacy wasn't just about the businesses or the profits—it was about the people. It was about the lives that had been changed, the doors that had been opened, and the generations of entrepreneurs who would continue to build on the foundation's principles.

A New Chapter

As the event came to a close, Alex found himself standing outside in the cool evening air. The city stretched before him, and he realized how much it had transformed since he first started his journey. The skyline had changed, but so had the world. The foundation's work had sparked a movement—a movement that was now beginning to flourish globally.

He thought back to the very beginning of his journey—the small apartment, the struggles, the doubts. But all of that had led him to this point. Every challenge, every setback, had been a stepping stone, pushing him toward the bigger picture. And now, he saw that the foundation's impact had already stretched far beyond what he had ever imagined.

The Full Circle Foundation wasn't just a project—it was a movement. And it was continuing to grow, evolve, and change the world for the better.

As he stood there, Alex felt a deep sense of fulfillment. His journey had come full circle, but it was far from over. The foundation would continue to thrive, expanding its reach and helping to shape the future of countless young entrepreneurs. The ripple effect would continue for generations to come, creating a legacy that was bigger than one person, bigger than one company. It was a legacy that would live on in the people who had been empowered to chase their dreams and make a difference in the world.

And with that thought, Alex knew that his work was far from finished. The legacy was continuing, evolving, and expanding—and it was in the hands of those he had mentored, those who would carry the torch forward, just as he had done for them.

The Lasting Impact

As the years went by, the Full Circle Foundation's reach only grew stronger. New mentors, alumni, and partners joined the cause, each bringing their unique expertise and passion for creating social change. The entrepreneurial hubs Alex had envisioned were now a reality, providing local communities with access to the tools, resources, and networks they needed to thrive.

Alex never stopped being involved in the foundation's work, but he stepped back from the day-to-day operations, trusting his team to carry the vision forward. He continued to mentor select individuals, offering guidance when needed, but he had learned the most important lesson of all—that the true power of mentorship was not in doing everything yourself, but in empowering others to lead.

And so, the legacy of the Full Circle Foundation continued to flourish, touching the lives of countless individuals who were now empowered to create businesses that would change the world for the better. The ripple effect that Alex had set into motion had only just begun.

THE END

www.ingramcontent.com/pod-product-compliance
Lightning Source LLC
Chambersburg PA
CBHW082250220526
45469CB00009B/2947